The Guilt
The Shame
and
The Blood

The Guilt
The Shame
and
The Blood

Michelle Steele

Copyright © 2011 Michelle Steele
Published by Faith Builders International
De Soto, Kansas 66018
Printed in the United States of America
ISBN 9780983599814

Dedication

I am forever grateful to my Substitute, Savior, and Lord, Jesus Christ. May this book be an instrument of freedom in His hands for all who read these pages. I will gladly become transparent for Your glory.

To my husband, Philip, I thank you for loving me, for building my faith, and being my stable, unchanging, forever friend. May this book reveal the inner healing your love has brought into my life.

To my children Jessica, Gene and Angela, I believe in each of you. Since I have known the Lord, I have taken His Word and framed your future. I declare, "Great is your peace with nothing missing and nothing broken!" Each of you brings a joy and delight to my life in your own unique way.

To my partners and the members of my congregation, thank you for being faith-builders! Together we will capture the attention of the lost, point them to Jesus Christ, and see many come to Him. I stand with you rejoicing in the victory of our Lord and Savior.

Table of Contents

1
The Guilt and the Shame

One Valium . . . are you kidding me? It would take a lot more than that for me to escape the reality of what I was doing. *That's alright* I told myself. I had just filled the prescription of Atavin that we got from the doctor, and I wasn't selling them this time. I planned to use them all during this time that I would be off "work." Along with the large bag of pot—and my plans to score a Dilaudid—I felt like I could escape the pain. The subconscious preparation was evidence that I knew this was the worst decision I had ever made.

My deluded reasoning kept me headed in that direction. What choice did I really have? I couldn't afford to be pregnant again. I had two children that somebody else was raising. They knew that I was their mom, but their grandma was the one who cooked their meals, washed their clothes, and gave them their baths. Even during the times that I lived in the same house with them, I didn't take care of them. I didn't buy their clothes or fix their hair. From the time that they were old enough to remember, my kids knew "Mom" as a woman who left in the afternoon and slept all day. I had given both of them over to "Grandma's" care just a few weeks after their birth so that I could return to work.

This work was part of my problem. I was a prostitute. I worked for an escort agency sometimes. At other times, I sold my body in the truck stop or on the streets of Nashville, Tennessee. As a prostitute, I was often pressured by men to allow unprotected sex for extra cash. Knowing that I had accepted a few of these offers—and also that there were times the condoms broke—I had no idea whose baby this was. With my other two children, there was no mistake. I wasn't actively prostituting during those conceptions. There was no "Momma's baby and Daddy's maybe" situation. One glance at those babies was all it took for the family to accept them.

I was afraid of the man that I was married to. Most of the people in East Nashville were afraid of him. I was afraid of losing him. I was afraid of making him angry. I was afraid that I would never see my children again. *He will kill me!* I thought to myself. If I gave birth to a baby that wasn't his, it would be trouble for me. Right now, I was valuable to him. He needed me. I did what he asked. I gave him all the money that I made. What a dilemma! He expected me to go out and have sex with other men for money; but the pressure was on me to keep from getting pregnant.

I was the one who found the clinic. I saved up the money. I stored up a supply of drugs. I made the appointment and told him what I had to do. I never told him about the broken condoms or times I had accepted extra money for sex without a condom. He didn't ask why I wanted an abortion. I explained that I couldn't work for a few weeks. He planned to take me to his mother's trailer out in the country.

That was the last place that I wanted to be. I spent my life sleeping all day and hooking all night and staying high in between. I didn't want to be reminded of the life that I really wanted. I didn't want to be reminded of a normal life where the husband worked and the wife cleaned and cooked. I didn't want to remember the dream of having a home and a family while recovering from an abortion.

The day of the procedure, we checked out of the cheap, weekly-rental motel on Dickerson Road. I was angry, but I tried not to show it. I hated him for putting me in this situation. I hated myself for staying in the situation. I was angry with myself for being such a weak woman. The only way I could deal with my shame and guilt was to turn it into anger. I answered him sharply knowing that at any minute he might slap my face. I didn't care.

He drove me to the clinic located a few blocks away in an industrial park. There were very few signs on the white, cinder-block building to advertise what really took place in there. He dropped me off with no interest in providing comfort or condolence. He didn't ask me, "Are you going to be okay?" or "Can you do this alone?" He just dropped me off with instructions for me to call him at his grandmother's house when I was done. I kept reminding myself that I didn't care. It just fueled my anger more to think that I had to do this alone.

A woman dressed in scrubs and a white lab coat took me into a room and handed me a Valium. I almost laughed in her face. One Valium isn't going to change anything. I wanted to put a needle in my arm and make this whole thing disappear. That was my method for calming my nerves. I shot cocaine for fun. But, I really liked the Dilaudid because it was instant pain relief. I could crush that little fifty-dollar pill, mix it with warm water in the syringe, and leave all the shame, humiliation, and degradation behind. After a shot, I could face the world— once I quit throwing up and scratching my nose. But, at that moment, all I had was one little Valium.

I took the Valium and chewed it up so that it would quickly get into my bloodstream. The woman handed me a paper gown and led me to a room without any eye contact or verbal interaction. I changed into the paper gown and lay on the cold table shivering and waiting.

My emotions went into a comatose state. Nothing mattered. That was how I had dealt with every bad decision that I had ever made. An emotional coma kept me from thinking about losing all contact with my parents when I ran away from home. An emotional coma kept me from suffering through the days of watching someone else raise my children. This coma guarded me when I had to walk

11

into dark hotel rooms or climb into a stranger's car. This emotional coma kept me from feeling the humiliation of having sex with men old enough to be my grandfather. This coma came to my rescue again as an uncaring, faceless doctor came into the room.

I felt the baby leave my body. That was the moment that I knew I had killed my unborn child. It wasn't just a fetus. It wasn't just a blob. Although I did not look, I knew. I have never forgotten that moment. I have never forgotten that feeling. There was no rewind button to reverse that moment. There was no one there to turn to and say, "What have I done!" Unlike the birth of my other children that was attended by the whole family, the death of my third child was a lonely event.

The whole procedure was over within five minutes. When the doctor left the room it was as nonchalantly as he had entered just a few minutes before. I was left alone and empty. I felt emptier than I had ever felt in my life. I cried empty tears. I wiped my empty eyes. I dressed in my jeans and sweatshirt and looked into the mirror over the small sink in the bathroom. There was no makeup to hide my emptiness. I hated myself more than ever at that moment.

I sat in the waiting room for the required time to ensure that the bleeding was not excessive. I called the man I was married to so that he could come pick me up. When he pulled up, he was already high. He never asked me how I was. He handed me a joint, and we prepared to head to his mother's house down in West Tennessee. I took a handful of Ativans. I just wanted to escape the guilt and shame.

Guilt was a constant companion in my life. The guilt produced a constant flow of shame that seeped into every area of my life. Like a poison, the shame slowly destroyed my self-esteem, my self-perception, my relationships, and every other part of my life.

It was like a vicious circle. Guilt was the awareness of my wrongdoing. Shame was the feeling or consciousness caused by the wrongdoing. The shame with its torment and degradation motivated me to more wrongdoing. Constantly, shame was talking and reasoning with me that I was dirty, guilty, and worthless. Shame campaigned with a relentless fury to convince me to self-destruct. Because of shame, I would stick a needle in my arm. Because of shame, I would leave my children with other people and walk the streets of Nashville, Tennessee. Shame multiplied my guilt and guilt multiplied my shame.

I had no clue what was really going on in my life. I had no idea that life was living me. Like a broken branch swept away in swollen stream, I was drowning in my decisions and their repercussions. From the years of teenage rebellion that ended in my running away from home to the life of drugs and crime that I was living, my life was a series of wrong turns and bad decisions. I was living in the "fast lane," yet the dead end was quickly approaching.

I remember thinking, "I have no other options. This is my life." I had no dream of a better life. I had no hope that I would have a beautiful house and loving family. I had no hope that I would have a savings account or retirement fund. I never even thought about growing old. I guess I never expected to live that long. I had given up on all of those dreams. Every bridge I crossed, I burned behind me. Every self-destructive decision backed me into another corner. I didn't think I could get help from my parents, I never thought about anyone in the community helping me. I definitely never thought about turning to God or asking for His help. I believed God hated me.

God knew everything. He knew all of the things I had hidden from my parents. He knew about the men I had been with and the unspeakable things I agreed to do. God knew about every item I ever shoplifted. He knew about the needles full of cocaine I had put in my arms and the pistol I carried in my purse. How could I ever turn to God? I was guilty; and I deserved everything God was going to do to me.

Just like the first man and woman on the earth, I was trying to avoid facing God. Shame was prompting me to cover myself like Adam and Eve attempted to do with those itchy fig leaves. The guilt of their action produced a shame in Adam and Eve that caused them to hide from their only source of help. They did not have what they needed to cover the guilt. They tried to deal with guilt on their own terms. It was failure. God had to help them confront their guilt. I couldn't keep hiding from the only One who could help me.

The guilt in my life was something I could hide from others. While everyone could see the effect of my guilt (i.e. addiction, violence, crime, etc.) they couldn't see the guilt that was piled up against me. I could keep on pretending that this lifestyle was what I wanted. I could convince others that I was living the way I wanted to live. I was parading around in my fig leaves like a fool.

Guilt is like a debt. When a person is guilty of a crime, there is a debt he or she owes to society. Our justice system requires that person to serve a sentence. My sin was a crime in a spiritual sense. I knew I was a "spiritual criminal." I was on the run from the spiritual law. I was a renegade. I was running because I couldn't pay the price for what I had done. I was running because I was trying to buy more time. But, I knew the day would come. So, I stayed high every waking moment to avoid the pain.

I knew I would go to hell when I died. I had no way to avoid it. Even if I quit every bad thing I was doing, I still had to deal with all of the things I had already done. It was impossible. I resolved in my mind and in my heart to accept the fate. I made jokes about it. I would say, "When I get to hell, I'm going to teach the devil a thing or two." I embraced the "bad girl" image, satanic music, and the extreme party-girl lifestyle.

I didn't know the words "sin" or "righteousness." I didn't understand what the word "salvation" meant. The word "delivered" was only used to describe pizza or mail as far as I was concerned. My life was void of any understanding or comprehension of God's real character or any options He had prepared for me. I was clueless, hopeless, and on the run.

Options? What options did I have? Guilt said, "You must pay." Shame said, "You can never pay for what you've done! Just run from it. Turn another trick and get high." I believed this lie for so long. I obeyed the instructions of shame and sunk deeper and deeper into a pit of addiction. My first overdose didn't slow me down. Facing the charges for three counts of attempted armed robbery didn't stop the downward spiral. When my husband died of an overdose, the downward spiral became a whirlwind of destruction. I lost custody of my children. I was sleeping on the streets. I didn't care about living.

Then, I found out about the option God had prepared for me. I heard that God had a way to remove my guilt. God wanted to totally forgive me of every single thing I had ever done and it would be like I never had sinned. At first I thought it was too good to be true. I was so hardened in my heart to any hope. When I prayed, there was only a small glimmer of hope.

Could it be true that God's only Son, Jesus Christ died in my place? I was a rebellious daughter. I was a miserable excuse for a mother. I was a junkie who cared more about her next high than anything else. I was a prostitute who would do just about anything for a few dollars. Why would Jesus die for me?

How could His death change my situation? I found out that Jesus had blood that was different than the blood of any person on the planet. Jesus had blood with no trace of sin in it. Jesus carried the blood of His Father, God. Jesus wasn't connected to the lineage of Adam with his inheritance of sin. Instead, Jesus was free from sin. He was tempted in every way that a person can be tempted, but He never sinned. This qualified His blood as the most valuable blood in the universe. It was valuable enough to pay my sin debt.

Guilt and sin demanded a life. God's law required it. That was the debt that I owed. I owed my life. Jesus didn't deserve to die. He was guiltless. He didn't owe any debt for sin. Yet, Jesus was willing to trade His life in exchange for mine. He was willing to die in order to pay my debt. His sinless blood contained His life. He poured His blood out to pay the price for every spiritual crime I ever committed.

God had prepared an option for me! There was a way for me to escape the cycle of guilt and shame. All I had to do was accept what Jesus did for me. To accept this, I had to believe in my heart that when Jesus hung on the cross, He was there in my place. I had to believe His blood was valuable enough to pay the price for my guilt.

This meant I was wrong about God all along. All of the time, I thought God hated me and was ready to punish me for my life. I was wrong! If God sent Jesus to die for me, that meant God loved me all along. He was willing to forgive me at any moment. I just had to come to Him through the way He had prepared. I had to follow the only path where I could remove the guilt from my life. God couldn't accept my guilt. But He prepared the payment for my guilt.

I prayed with that faint glimmer of hope in my heart. Although my life didn't magically transform, my heart did. Over the next few weeks and months, God sent people into my life who taught me about God's character and His Word. It was definitely a process of transformation. God changed my life. The transformation began with Jesus blood removing my guilt. [1]

---

[1] For more details about my life story, read *Walking in the Graveyard*.

2
Guilty as Charged

I love true stories of people overcoming adversity. People respond to victims and their heart-wrenching tales of enduring abuse or escaping from an attack. As difficult as it is for the victim to relive the details of their experience, it is easier to tell the victim's story than to tell the story of the guilty party.

The story of guilt is harder to hear and more difficult to tell. The guilty person has no one in the audience willing to share compassion. They have no one to extend arms of comfort or wipe away the tears as if to say, "It is going to be alright." The audience is judging their actions, motives, and outcome. They usually have no excuse or reason to validate what they have done. They are guilty.

Sitting in church for the first few years after Jesus saved me and delivered me from drugs, I was listening for a true story from someone who was once guilty. I heard the stories of many victims, and I rejoiced with them for their rescue. I cried with the people who survived. I celebrated their healing and restoration from the abuse and pain. But, I didn't completely relate to them.

I told parts of my pain. Speaking of the details that related to the victim side of my experience, I shared edited versions of my story leaving out the guilty details. I was hoping to tell enough to qualify me for acceptance without telling the parts that could cause my rejection. I didn't want to be the outcast or the black sheep of the church. I assumed that all of the people in the church were perfect and sheltered. They wouldn't understand my arrest record. They wouldn't relate to my lies, crimes, or addictions.

When I actually started reading the Bible, I was shocked and relieved. In the Bible there are true stories of people who were liars, cheaters, and murderers. God still had a plan for their lives! I found a man in the Bible who admitted to the extreme guilt of his past without fear of rejection. Paul told his story without excuse and without qualm. He said things like, "I am the chief of sinners" (1 Timothy 1:15). I could relate with that! Finally, somebody was speaking my language.

This man Paul became an apostle who wrote two-thirds of the New Testament. God used Paul as an instrument of revelation knowledge. Through Paul, Jesus established the knowledge of who we are in Christ and the victory we have in Jesus Christ by grace. The growth of the church was greatly affected by this man.

Paul was on a ship during a terrible storm. The ship fell apart during the storm, and all of the people on the ship floated to the shore of an island. The inhabitants of the island built a fire to warm the survivors. Paul helped to gather sticks for the fire and, as he threw some of the sticks on the fire, a venomous snake came out of the fire and bit him. Let's look at this story from *The Amplified Bible.*

After we were safe on the island, we knew and recognized that it was called Malta. And the natives showed us unusual and remarkable kindness, for they kindled a fire and welcomed and received us all, since it had begun to rain and was cold. Now Paul had gathered a bundle of sticks, and he was laying them on the fire when a viper crawled out because of the heat and fastened itself on his hand. When the natives saw the little animal hanging from his hand, they said to one another, "Doubtless this man is a murderer, for though he has been saved from the sea, Justice [the goddess of avenging] has not permitted that he should live." Then [Paul simply] shook off the small creature into the fire and suffered no evil effects (Acts 28:1-5 AMP).

These villagers believed in "justice." In their minds, they surmised since Paul survived the shipwreck only to be bitten by a viper, he must have done something so terrible that justice was "catching up with him." They said, "This man must be a murderer!" They believed that Paul was getting what he deserved because of the actions of his past.

The interesting thing to consider is this: Paul testified about his past in Acts 26. Before Paul accepted Jesus as his Lord, he was named Saul. He made it his business to destroy the Christians.

> I myself indeed was [once] persuaded that it was my duty to do many things contrary to and in defiance of the name of Jesus of Nazareth. And that is what I did in Jerusalem; I [not only] locked up many of the [faithful] saints (holy ones) in prison by virtue of authority received from the chief priests, but when they were being condemned to death, I cast my vote against them. And frequently I punished them in all the synagogues to make them blaspheme; and in my bitter fury against them, I harassed (troubled, molested, persecuted) and pursued them even to foreign cities (Acts 26:9-11 AMP).

In verse 10, Paul said he had a part in the deaths of innocent people. He helped to kill people just because they believed in Jesus Christ as their Lord and Savior. With the right attorney, we could have Saul convicted as an accessory to murder in our court system today! Saul was a murderer. He admitted his guilt. Look at this verse from another translation.

> I locked many Christians in prison. I voted to have them killed every time a vote was taken (Acts 26:10 GW).

Saul voted "Kill them" every time. Saul was there when Stephen was stoned to death. *The Amplified Bible* says in Acts 28:1, "And Saul was not only consenting to Stephen's death, he was pleased and entirely approving. . . ." In verse three of that same chapter it says:

> But Saul shamefully treated and laid waste the church continuously [with cruelty and violence]; and entering house after house, he dragged out men and women and committed them to prison (Acts 8:3).

This man experienced more than just a name change when he submitted to the Lord Jesus Christ. Paul didn't carry the guilt of his actions. He didn't relate with his past. He could testify and declare, "I was guilty as charged" on one hand and on the other hand declare, "I am innocent." Paul made a statement in 2 Corinthians that indicates he isn't connected to the guilt of his past.

> Receive us; we have wronged no man, we have corrupted no man, we have defrauded no man (2 Corinthians 7:2).

How could Paul say this? The connection between his past and his present had been severed so completely the guilt of his actions could no longer reach him. If Paul still lived in the shadow of his guilt, he would have thought about the accusation of the people on the island. He would have considered the idea that his past cruelty was coming back to haunt him. Paul might have thought *I was a murderer. I deserve to die.* But instead Paul shook off the snake and went on his way.

— I believed I was forgiven. But, I still carried a lot of shame for the things I had done and the way I had lived. Perhaps, my problem was in my definition of forgiveness. Maybe I needed a greater understanding of the complete work Jesus had done I my life. Whatever the reason, I spent many years as a Christian with shame and humiliation hiding in my conscious.

In old spy movies, story lines featured people who had been programmed to assassinate or commit crimes. They were programmed or brainwashed to respond to certain words. When these words were spoken, they would immediately go into action and carry out the crime. These people would live their everyday lives and carry on with normal activity. All of the time, there was a hidden, dangerous command planted in their subconscious. When the time was right, they became a pawn in the hands of the one who had planted the idea in their mind. In that same way, shame had been planted in my consciousness and was lying dormant as I carried out my life as a Christian.

The shame of my past actions became a strategic weapon for the enemy to paralyze my faith. Like that hidden command planted in the mind of that unknowing person, the shame was a destructive, volatile explosive waiting for the right circumstance and condition to be activated. I was clueless to its presence.

I was living my life for the first time in years. God was rebuilding what I had spent twenty-three years destroying. After the death of my first husband, I lost custody of my children. My drug addiction became so extreme that I overdosed and was brought back to life with CPR. When Jesus came into my life, there was nothing of value I had wasted anything of worth.

After Jesus saved me from that graveyard of addiction and prostitution, I regained custody of my children. Jessica and Gene moved in with me into a small apartment in Madison, Tennessee. Jessica was six-years-old and Gene four-years-old. I had never been a mother to them. I had never been a disciplinarian or a comforter, but they were so loving and willing to forget the years of my absence.

With a lot of help from the people of our church and some miracles from God, I regained my driver's license and received furniture for my apartment. I was learning how to be a mom for the first time in my life. Shopping, cleaning, and organizing a home were all new experiences.

God brought into my life the man of my dreams: a strong, devoted husband and father with God's call clearly on his life. In my time of prayer, I had prayed for a husband. My specific requests to God included a man who would be stronger than me in the Word of God to lead me, a man who would love my children like his own, and a man who would praise and worship God without reservation. Philip was everything I asked for and much more.

Philip loved my children like they were his own. Jessica and Gene called him "Daddy" from the beginning. He would play with the children making imaginary stories with the G.I. Joes and stuffed animals. They wrestled and played on the merry-go-round at the park. Life had never been so full and peaceful.

It seemed like a dream-come-true! In the first year of our marriage I discovered I was pregnant. We were expecting our first child together! What a great direction for our new life! I had such an excitement. Things were so different in my life. There were no drugs or alcohol. I could enjoy and share this experience with Philip. I could enjoy bringing a new life into the world, a life that represented our love.

Philip and I didn't care what other people thought about the fact that we were going to have another child added to our ready-made family. We started planning. We spent hours discussing different name choices and wondering if we would have a boy or a girl. We shared the news with the children to prepare them for their new baby brother or sister. Our life was picture-perfect.

Then, one day I noticed a dark, brown, faint flow of blood. When I mentioned it to my sister-in-law, her face fell in horror. Since I hadn't seen a doctor yet for prenatal care, she made an emergency appointment for me at a doctor's office. Philip was at work cleaning cars in his brother-in-law's detail shop when I called to tell him that I was on my way to the doctor's office. I stopped by the detail shop on my way, and we prayed together. Philip was so positive. He encouraged me to think the best. The whole way to the doctor's office while I was hoping for the best, the shame lying dormant in my consciousness began to awaken.

In the back of my mind, I began to hear a thought that was not born from my time reading God's Word. It didn't originate from the teaching of my pastors. It wasn't a thought that agreed with anything in my new Christian life. It was a haunting thought buried for years in my mind waiting for the perfect moment to sabotage my faith when I needed it most. I thought about the abortion from years ago and the shame came flooding into my heart.

I wanted to believe in the God of miracles that had rescued me from an addiction that destroyed so many others. I had seen God do great things to restore and rebuild my life. I knew that He was able to save my baby. But my faith was hindered by my shame. I thought *I am losing this baby because I killed my last child. I don't deserve to have this baby because I didn't value the life of my last child. I am reaping what I sowed. Something is probably wrong with my uterus because of that abortion.*

The Bible promises this in Ephesians 3:

Now unto him that is able to do exceeding
abundantly above all that we ask or think, according
to the power that worketh in us (Ephesians 3:20).

God had the ability to save my baby. I know He wanted to stop what was happening. But the only power working in me was the shame from my guilt. Faith requires righteousness to be at work in your heart. I had no righteousness to stand on because I felt so guilty. God couldn't help me because I disconnected from His power and began focusing on the guilt of the things He had already forgiven me. Fear and shame robbed my faith of the strength necessary to receive from God.

Just like those people on the island of Melita, who watched a man survive a shipwreck only to be bitten by a venomous viper, I thought that justice had caught up with me. My defenses fell. I placed my shield of faith to the side and began to weep with those same empty, shame-filled tears from my past. The doctor searched for a heartbeat to no avail. As he pointed out the form of my lifeless child on the screen of the ultrasound machine, those empty, haunting tears from my past wandered down my face.

Philip came to my side as I went through the process to remove the baby from my uterus. Sorrow and shame gave way to grief as I realized my child was dead. Miscarriage is the death of a child you love. My baby had a name. My baby already had a place in my heart although I would never hold him in my arms.

In a miscarriage, there is no funeral or casket. People act like you are overreacting because the baby wasn't fully formed or ready to be born. The grief is just as real. The loss of a life is just as real. It can be so confusing because people expect the parents to just forget about this loss. I couldn't just forget.

I grieved in silence while my husband went on a spiritual search. Philip wanted answers. People tried to console us by saying things like, "We don't know why God allows things like this . . . " or "We can't explain why God did this." Philip refused to accept these statements at face value. He prayed and searched God's Word. He opened his heart to God and made a decision. He came into our room one morning after prayer and took me gently by my hands. He said, "I can't explain why this happened, but I know it was not God's fault. Jesus gives life and abundant life. The enemy is the one responsible for killing, stealing, and destroying. We were attacked by the devil, and we lost that fight. It won't happen again! We are going to trust God and shut any door to the enemy." We prayed together and resolved that we wouldn't lose another battle.

At the time, I never recognized the presence of shame and the part it had played in my situation. Years later, as I developed the force of righteousness in my spirit, I realized the shame that had operated behind the scenes. I saw all of the prayers that were weighed down and made useless through the shame. The shame was trespassing. Its presence was illegal. Yet, I didn't recognize and resist the shame.

3
The Dangers of Shame

The reason I am sharing some of the most transparent moments of my life is to help someone else recognize and escape the destruction of shame. Perhaps you have a family member or friend who is running from reality through drug addiction, bulimia, or anorexia. Maybe you keep destroying everything good in your life and then bury yourself in food or alcohol to comfort the pain that is multiplying in your life. You don't have to ride this roller coaster of pain and misery. God has a freedom for you.

1. Hiding from Our Help

Shame will cause you to hide or withdraw from the people who love you the most. I mentioned the first shame recorded in the history of mankind was from the life of Adam and Eve. The first couple once anticipated their long, peaceful walks with their Father God in the Garden of Eden. Now, when God comes to visit, He calls and searches for them. Adam and Eve are hiding from the One who genuinely loves and cares for them. The reason they had guilt was because of what they had done. They disobeyed God. Their guilt caused shame to sweep over their emotions and perceptions. They were guilty, but they felt the shame. The shame is the painful feeling of remorse and regret. It hurts. Our first and natural reaction is to escape or hide from the pain that shame causes.

Peter was suffering the shame of denying Jesus. I am sure that Peter thought he would exceed all of the disciples in his zeal and courage. When the soldiers came rushing in to take Jesus into custody, Peter pulled his sword and cut the ear off of one of the soldiers. He may not have been a polished swordsman but he was ready to fight for Jesus.

Peter was quick to tell Jesus, "I will lay down my life for your sake." Jesus said, "Oh, really?" Look at the conversation from *The Amplified Bible.*

Peter said to Him, Lord, why cannot I follow You now? I will lay down my life for You. Jesus answered, Will you [really] lay down your life for Me? I assure you, most solemnly I tell you, before a rooster crows, you will deny Me [completely disown Me] three times (John 13:37-38 AMP).

This was not what Peter expected to hear. Peter never planned to completely disown Jesus. Peter had high hopes and dreams of his ability to represent Jesus. He wanted to showcase what the Master had taught him. But, when Jesus was being questioned and tortured, Peter was in the courtyard of the palace pretending that he didn't know Jesus. He even cussed to prove to the people standing around him that he was not with Jesus.

Then Peter began to invoke a curse on himself and to swear, I do not even know the Man! And at that moment a rooster crowed. And Peter remembered Jesus' words, when He had said, Before a single rooster crows, you will deny and disown Me three times. And he went outside and wept bitterly (Matthew 26:74-75 AMP).

Have you ever done something that you thought you would never do? Have you ever found yourself in this place of failure? Peter was disgusted with himself. He was ashamed of his actions and weakness. At the moment, when Jesus needed him the most, Peter failed him. Mark 14:72 records:

"When he thought thereon, he wept" (KJV).

The *God's Word* translation says, "Then, Peter began to cry very hard."

The Message paraphrase reads, "He collapsed in tears."

The New Living Translation records, "And he broke down and wept."

In the book of Luke, we have an important detail of this moment. The Lord Jesus Christ looked at Peter at the moment of the disciple's failure. Can you imagine the shame that Peter felt at that moment?

> And the Lord turned and looked at Peter. And Peter recalled the Lord's words, how He had told him, Before the cock crows today, you will deny Me thrice. And he went out and wept bitterly [that is, with painfully moving grief] (Luke 22:61-62).

– The next recorded conversation between Peter and Jesus is a conversation dealing with Peter's shame. This is the third time Jesus has appeared to His disciples. But, it is the first recorded interaction between Peter and Jesus since his failure. Jesus found His disciples fishing on the sea of Tiberias. He ministers to them with an abundant supply of fish. He had prepared a fire with fish and bread and called them to come eat. After the meal, Jesus reaches out to Peter. When you read the whole story, you sense Peter holding back. There is no indication that Peter rushed to Jesus' side or wrapped his arms around Jesus in a big hug Peter pulled in the net of fish while everyone else went to see Jesus.

– Jesus helped Peter work through the three times he had denied Him. The Lord knew Peter had to confront the shame of his failure in order to restore the relationship and fulfill his future. Jesus asked Peter, "Do you love me?" The Lord asked him the same question three times. For the three times Peter denied the Lord, he was able to confess his love for Jesus. Immediately after the declaration of His love for the Master, Jesus was able to talk about Peter's destiny. The shame was hiding Peter's view of the future and destiny.

This shows me Jesus wants to teach us to confront the guilt and deal with the shame before the shame separates us from our help. Most people have never been taught to confront their mistakes. We have hidden, buried, and avoided the real issue until the poison of our pain became bitterness. Marriages are falling apart because of shame from our childhood. Parents are passing insecurities and resentment onto their children because they are full of guilt from failures they have never confronted. We must confront the real issues and let Jesus walk us through the process like He did for Peter. Each one of us has a destiny and purpose in God that requires a healthy, shame-free relationship with the Lord Jesus Christ.

2. Self-Destruction

Compare the shame of Peter to the shame of Judas. Both men experienced a great failure. Judas betrayed Jesus with a kiss of friendship.

> As He was still speaking, Judas, one of the Twelve [apostles], came up, and with him a great crowd with swords and clubs, from the chief priests and elders of the people. Now the betrayer had given them a sign, saying, The One I shall kiss is the Man; seize Him. And he came up to Jesus at once and said, Hail (greetings, good health to You, long life to You), Master! And he embraced Him and kissed Him with [pretended] warmth and devotion. Jesus said to him, Friend, for what are you here? Then they came up and laid hands on Jesus and arrested Him (Matthew 26:47-50 AMP).

I believe that God's grace was bigger than Judas' failure. I trust that the blood Jesus poured out to pay for my sin could have removed Judas' sin and cleansed him of the shame. Shame drove Judas away from all his friends. Shame drove Judas to the wrong source for his comfort. He went back to the people who had used him and taken advantage of him.

> Then Judas, which had betrayed him, when he saw that he was condemned, repented himself, and brought again the thirty pieces of silver to the chief priests and elders, Saying, I have sinned in that I have betrayed the innocent blood. And they said, What is that to us? see thou to that. And he cast down the pieces of silver in the temple, and departed, and went and hanged himself (Matthew 27:3-5).

This is what shame can drive a person to do. Judas killed himself before anyone had a chance to reach him with the truth about mercy. Shame convinced Judas that every door was shut for him. He didn't reach out to anyone who could have helped him. He hid from anyone who had help for him. He shut out the world. Judas went into self-destruct mode. He killed himself while drowning in the despair of what he had done.

Judas walked with Jesus. He heard the best sermons Jesus ever taught. He heard Jesus teach about the anointing to remove burdens and destroy yokes or bondages. Judas knew Jesus preached a message of mercy. Judas watched Jesus treat with compassion the woman caught in adultery. Judas knew the Lord and was anointed by the Master. Guilt and shame drove Judas away from the Lord like guilt and shame separated the first man from his Creator. With Judas, the self-destruction was quick.

Addiction is a slow death. Anorexia is painful, gradual form of self-destruction. Cutting or self-mutilation is an outward release of an inner pain that continues to spread. It is never enough. Self-destruction never reaches a point where we think, "I have suffered enough." While we think self-destruction is our self-punishment, it is deception. It will continue until it takes the very life out of our being.

3. The Perception of Rejection

When guilt unleashes the shame into our lives, one response is to harden our heart against the remorse. I mentioned my "emotional coma" in the first chapter of this book. I hardened my heart. I buried my feelings. I told myself *You have to do what you have to do. Just get through this.* This was a culmination of years of telling myself *I did something to deserve this.*

You can have shame for things you didn't do. You can accept blame and carry the humiliation for things done to you that were out of your control. I was in junior high school when I was first molested. During a two-year time frame, there were three different men who took advantage of me. One was a football coach who taught my health class. One was the father of a classmate. The other was a man who managed the barn where I kept my horse. I never confronted them for the things they did to me. I never told anyone. I thought it was my fault. I accepted the blame. I began to see myself through a filter of rejection. I took the responsibility for what these adults had done and inflicted the punishment on myself.

That shame changed my perception of myself. I saw myself as "dirty." In my mind, there was something wrong with me that caused this to happen. It was during that time that I turned to music that talked about Satan and suicide. I locked myself in the bathroom and tried to cut my wrists. My parents couldn't figure out what was wrong with me. They placed me in the mental ward of St. Thomas hospital in Nashville, Tennessee. I visited with the psychiatrist every week. He placed me on anti-depressants and released me. I tried to kill myself by taking an entire bottle of the meds he had prescribed. I woke up the next day extremely sick. I didn't realize that I was self-destructing.

I started sleeping around with older boys. I no longer had a value system. I thought I had to use sex to get acceptance or attention. When I ran away, I was trying to gain the acceptance of a guy. It was like destruction had a target on my back. I was easy prey for anyone wanting to control me with the right manipulation. I perceived my world through a fear of rejection. I thought everyone could see what had happened to me and they would hate me for it.

I remember the conversation that led me to prostitution. I wanted this guy to love me. I wanted to please him. A year before, I broke him out of a juvenile detention center and ran across the country with him. When I became pregnant with his child, he dumped me. He ended up dating my "best friend" from junior high school. He was prostituting her in a massage parlor in East Nashville. They were shooting drugs and partying while I lived with his family and worked two restaurant jobs.

He came by his grandmother's house where I was living. I was about six months pregnant. He said, "If you want to be with me, you've got to do what she is doing." The more attention he gave me the more pressure I felt. I thought it was what I had to do. He flirted with me and sweet-talked me. I really wanted his approval. I had run away to be with him. The woman I am today would never have fallen for the manipulation I succumbed to on that day. Out of desperation to be accepted by him I agreed to prostitute.

At sixteen-years-old, while six-months pregnant, I climbed into an eighteen-wheeler and had sex for money. I spent the next seven years in every level of prostitution from the exclusive hotels in Nashville to the roughest streets like Murfreesboro Road and Dickerson Road. It was never easy. It was never fun. I learned to harden my heart to the humiliation. I learned to disengage my feelings from what I was doing. I thought *This is my life. Deal with it!*

A nameless woman who lived in Samaria had learned to desensitize herself to her lifestyle. Her story is told in John 4 of the Bible.

> And Jacob's well was there. So Jesus, tired as He was from His journey, sat down [to rest] by the well. It was then about the sixth hour (about noon). Presently, when a woman of Samaria came along to draw water, Jesus said to her, Give Me a drink (John 4:6-7 AMP).

I have heard different teachers explain the tradition of most women in the city was to draw their water early in the morning. This woman came to the well when she knew she would be alone. There is no one else there except Jesus. As the story continues, the truth comes out about this woman's lifestyle. When Jesus mentions her husband, the woman admits she doesn't have a husband.

> The woman answered, I have no husband. Jesus said to her, You have spoken truly in saying, I have no husband. For you have had five husbands, and the man you are now living with is not your husband. In this you have spoken truly (John 4:17-18 AMP).

The Bible doesn't say this woman was a prostitute, but we can tell she wasn't in the affluent, respected part of her community. She perceived herself as a reject and separated herself from the other women. She was used to condemnation. Her conversation with Jesus is sharp and biting. She is ready for a fight. She is ready for rejection.

Jesus wasn't condemning her. He was confronting her with truth. Just like God confronted Adam and Jesus confronted Peter, Jesus was confronting this woman for the purpose of helping her make a change. Jesus wants to help you. If we hide from the problem, it continues. It grows and destroys the good in our life. What you won't confront, you cannot change. It is time to take your guilt to God and confront it with His love. It is time to recognize if you are carrying guilt for what someone did to you. Don't continue to suffer for what another person did to you.

This Samaritan woman encountered God's love, and she was changed. She had spent years in failing relationships. She had endured days, weeks, and possibly years of loneliness and rejection. When Jesus helped her confront the issues, she was able to find joy and strength. She went through the town testifying about the Lord and spreading the news. Her main declaration was "Come see a man which told me all things I ever did: is not this the Christ?" She was amazed that Jesus would confront her without condemnation. The reference to Jesus being the Christ is a reference to the One who removes burdens and destroys the bondage. Jesus removed the guilt and destroyed the shame.

4
Your Guilt = My Shame

I want to go deeper in the exploration of shame that is brought on by the guilt of another person. Children who were molested are carrying the shame caused by the crime of their abuser. Women who were raped are carrying the fear and humiliation caused by the crime of their attacker. Wives whose husbands have brought pornography into their homes are filled with shame because they blame themselves for not being sexy enough to satisfy their man. Too many victims are struggling to carry the shame of a guilt that belongs to someone else. Too many lives are lost in torment because of what someone else decided to do.

One of the saddest stories in the Bible is about a young woman named Tamar.

Absalom son of David had a fair sister whose name was Tamar, and Amnon [her half brother] son of David loved her.
And Amnon was so troubled that he fell sick for his [half] sister Tamar, for she was a virgin, and Amnon thought it impossible for him to do anything to her.
But Amnon had a friend whose name was Jonadab son of Shimeah, David's brother, and Jonadab was a very crafty man.
He said to Amnon, Why are you, the king's son, so lean and weak-looking from day to day? Will you not tell me? And Amnon said to him, I love Tamar, my [half] brother Absalom's sister.
Jonadab said to him, Go to bed and pretend you are sick; and when your father David comes to see you, say to him, Let my sister Tamar come and give me

food and prepare it in my sight, that I may see it and eat it from her hand.

So Amnon lay down and pretended to be sick; and when the king came to see him, Amnon said to the king, I pray you, let my sister Tamar come and make me a couple of cakes in my sight, that I may eat from her hand.

Then David sent home and told Tamar, Go now to your brother Amnon's house and prepare food for him.

So Tamar went to her brother Amnon's house, and he was in bed. And she took dough and kneaded it and made cakes in his sight and baked them.

She took the pan and emptied it out before him, but he refused to eat. And Amnon said, Send everyone out from me. So everyone went out from him.

Then Amnon said to Tamar, Bring the food here into the bedroom, so I may eat from your hand. So Tamar took the cakes she had made and brought them into the room to Amnon her brother.

And when she brought them to him, he took hold of her and said, Come lie with me, my sister (2 Samuel 13:1-11 AMP).

Tamar is an innocent young woman with her entire life ahead of her. She comes to help her brother who is sick only to find out that she has been set up. The whole time it was really about getting her in this vulnerable position. While Amnon claims to love Tamar, it is not the kind of love that wants to protect or nurture. In reality, Amnon has a selfish desire. He wants Tamar with no consideration for her well-being or her future. Amnon raped her.

"No, my brother!" she cried. "Don't be foolish! Don't do this to me! Such wicked things aren't done in Israel. Where could I go in my shame? And you would be called one of the greatest fools in Israel. Please, just speak to the king about it, and he will let you marry me. But Amnon wouldn't listen to her, and since he was stronger than she was, he raped her (2 Samuel 13:12-14 NLT).

There was a perfectly acceptable way that Amnon could have been with his stepsister. He could have asked the king for permission to marry her. If Amnon really loved her, he could have spent the rest of his life with her as his wife. Amnon didn't care about Tamar. He only cared about himself.

Tamar knew she would carry the shame for this action. It was against her will. It was out of her control. It was something she could not stop from happening. Yet, her life would carry the mark of what her brother did to her. Look at the question Tamar asked of Amnon. "Where could I go in my shame?"

The *King James Version* says, "And I, whither shall I cause my shame to go?"

The *God's Word* translation records, "Where could I go in my disgrace?"

The Message paraphrase reads, "Where could I ever show my face?"

In the *Amplified Bible* it says, "And I, how could I rid myself of my shame?"

This is the question I want you to consider: How could I rid myself of my shame? Is that what is happening when a person inflicts self-punishment by cutting marks in her body or drowning himself in addiction? Are you trying to rid yourself of your shame? Like the victim of a rape who spends hours in the shower trying to wash off the inner filth they feel, you might try in your own power to remove the disgrace that is overwhelming you. It is impossible for you to rid yourself of any shame especially the shame that is a result of the guilt of another person.

41

What they did to you was wrong! It looks like they have gone on with their life and left you broken, shattered, and disgraced. It may not be fair. You may not have all of the answers that you think you need. "Why did this happen? Why me? What did I do to deserve this? Did I cause it? Is it my fault?" Asking the wrong questions only breeds frustration because you are missing the truth. The truth is this: There is an enemy, an adversary who has targeted you for destruction. God's enemy saw your potential. God's adversary recognized you and knew God's love for you.

Because we remind Satan of his enemy, we become a target for his destruction. He knows whose child we are. For instance, my daughter went to a youth meeting in a church where the pastors are my friends. Although my friend had never personally met my daughter, she knew exactly whose child that was. When Angela attended a conference where I was ministering, she had to go back to the hotel room for something she left behind. She climbed on the elevator and a woman from the conference said, "You must be Michelle Steele's daughter!" I wasn't standing there next to her, but because she looks so much like me, it is apparent she is my child.

There are things that happen to us because the enemy is trying to abort God's plan for your life long before you realize there is a plan. If the enemy can set you up for failure and plant some roadside bombs alongside the path to your purpose he can separate you from a relationship with God.

Joseph was thrown into a pit as a young boy. His brothers wanted to kill him, but they decided to sell him into slavery and tell their father Joseph was killed by animals. Joseph went as a slave into Egypt. He became the manager of the household for his master Potiphar. Potiphar's wife tried to seduce Joseph, and when he refused her, she accused him of trying to rape her. He was thrown into prison. All of his life he was treated unfairly. People lied on him. Those who should have loved him tried to kill him. This was supernatural! One attack after another was launched against Joseph. Do you really think these things just happened to him without an evil force motivating people behind the scenes? The attack was aimed at the purpose, destiny, and potential in Joseph. It was a strategic plan of the enemy to make Joseph useless and powerless. God needed Joseph to be a leader through the famine and help an entire nation through the worst struggle of their generation. The attack was intended to stop this purpose and to destroy the very lineage of Jesus Christ!

Every attack on your life is on purpose. The evil things you have endured are painful and degrading. These evil things were demonically inspired. The shame that causes you to cut, drink, or get high is fulfilling its designed purpose. The shame of that abuse is a weapon of the enemy. The adversary knows your potential. He recognizes something in you that he must stop. Shame is trying to hinder you.

Only God can rid you of shame. There is only one substance in the world with the cleansing agent to remove the stain of shame. Through the blood of Jesus Christ, God can remove the shame and totally remove the consciousness of your being a victim. When the blood of Jesus has cleansed you, you won't consider yourself to be a victim with no hope. You will perceive yourself clean. You will sense your destiny. You will be able to look ahead and move in the direction of your purpose. You have to go to God. Don't let the shame continue to separate you from God.

Don't blame God for what that person did. God didn't do it. I am done with people blaming God for what happened to me. Well-meaning people have patted my hand and said, "God allowed all of those terrible things to happen to you so He could use you for His glory now." I want to scream in their face, "No!" God didn't plan for men to molest me. God didn't want me to be a prostitute. It didn't please God for me to spend years lost in a cloudy haze of drug addiction just so I could testify to drug addicts. I would never let anything bad happen to my children so that they could be instrumental for me later. That would be child abuse!

God didn't allow or permit those things. God gave each person a free will. If a person commits a crime or violates the rights of another person, they chose to do it. God hated it when those men molested me. God hated it when grown men manipulated me and touched me in places that only my husband should touch me. It broke God's heart to see it happen. Unless those men repent and receive forgiveness for their guilt, God will punish them. But God didn't sit back and say, "Let it happen."

If you have spent years being angry with God, He is strong enough to endure your cold shoulder and still love you. But your help is in Him. The only hope you have of being free from the destruction and helplessness is in God through the blood of Jesus. Whatever you do, turn to Him. Trust Him. Let Him heal you and rid you of your shame.

Maybe You Were Dropped

There are many other examples in the Bible of people suffering from the actions and mistakes of others. Saul's disobedience inadvertently caused suffering and shame in the life of his own grandson, Mephibosheth. Because of the fall of Saul's kingdom, the woman caring for his grandson dropped him in her attempt to run away.

Jonathan, Saul's son, had a son who was a cripple in his feet. He was five years old when the news came out of Jezreel [of the deaths] of Saul and Jonathan. And the boy's nurse took him up and fled; and in her

haste, he fell and became lame. His name was
Mephibosheth (2 Samuel 4:4 AMP).

This boy's life went from best to worst in an instant. He
was the son of the prince in line for the throne. He was born
to be royalty. He lived in a palace with the world at his
fingertips. Because of the choices of other people, his
chance to rule the kingdom was ripped away from him. He
grew up like an orphan with no real family to cherish or
adore him. Because he was an heir to Saul's throne, his
nurse probably told him David would kill him if he ever
discovered he was alive. He was paralyzed because his
nurse dropped him. He was homeless, helpless, and
abandoned by society.
But, King David made a covenant with Mephibosheth's
father long before Jonathan was killed. His father, Jonathan
was David's best friend. David was searching for anyone in
Jonathan's family to show kindness to them.

The king said, Is there not still someone of the house
of Saul to whom I may show the [unfailing,
unsought, unlimited] mercy and kindness of God?
Ziba replied, Jonathan has yet a son who is lame in
his feet. And the king said, Where is he? Ziba replied,
He is in the house of Machir son of Ammiel in Lo-
debar (2 Samuel 9:3 4 AMP).

David didn't want to hurt Mephibosheth. He wanted to
help him. The servant, Ziba, told King David where
Mephibosheth was living. He was living in Lo-debar. The
name of this town is a Hebrew word that means "no
pasture, no word, or no communication." Mephibosheth
had shut himself off from communication with everyone.
He had no pasture or place of safety and provision. This
word Lo-debar can also be translated as "land of nothing."

Does that give you an idea of the empty, loneliness of this young man's life?

Because of the choices, actions, and mistakes of other people, Mephibosheth was living a life without provision. He had nothing and nobody. He was empty. Have you experienced disappointment because of the mistakes of someone else in your life? Maybe your husband decided to throw away your marriage after thirty years. Are you are raising your teenager's child? Perhaps your company went bankrupt, and you lost your retirement fund. Whatever the scenario—if you are weighted down with shame and humiliation because of your actions or the actions of other people—your King Jesus is searching for you. He wants to show you the kindness of God. He wants to take you from the land of nothing and bring you to the king's table of provision.

> So David sent for him and brought him from Makir's home. His name was Mephibosheth; he was Jonathan's son and Saul's grandson. When he came to David, he bowed low to the ground in deep respect. David said, "Greetings, Mephibosheth." Mephibosheth replied, "I am your servant." "Don't be afraid!" David said. "I intend to show kindness to you because of my promise to your father, Jonathan. I will give you all the property that once belonged to your grandfather Saul, and you will eat here with me at the king's table!" Mephibosheth bowed respectfully and exclaimed, "Who is your servant, that you should show such kindness to a dead dog like me?" (2 Samuel 9:5-8 NLT).

Look at the perception Mephibosheth has about himself! He calls himself a "dead dog." The idea of worthlessness and the expectation of rejection have affected the way he views his world. Sadly, this is the perception that many people have about themselves. People allow their condition to identify them. People find their value or lack of value in the opinions of others or by the treatment they have received from other people.

Your circumstance is not supposed to tell you who you are. If you allow your circumstance to identify you, you become a victim to the circumstance. You will be stranded in that circumstance. You are not what you did and you are not what happened to you. You can rise above your situation. You can take God's weapons and obliterate shame and fear from your life. You are who God says you are. You are fearfully and wonderfully made. Your Creator is the only One qualified to identify you.

Mephibosheth had difficulty receiving kindness. He was accustomed to treatment that reinforced the low self-esteem and perception of shame. Have you ever met a man or woman who stays with someone who verbally or physically abuses them? You can ask that person, "Why do you stay with them and let them treat you like that?" That treatment is what they think they deserve. There are multitudes of people who remain in volatile relationships because that is the treatment they are accustomed to. They gravitate toward the people who take advantage of them and disrespect them. It is difficult for that person to receive compliments or kindness.

At some point in our lives, we have to recover from all the times other people have dropped us. We have to take the control of our destiny out of the hands of the people who failed us and put that control in the hands of Jesus Christ. He is the only One qualified to direct our lives. Jesus is the perfect Lord for your life. He will never drop you! He will never take your life in the direction of failure, pain, or destruction. Jesus will never fail you or break your trust. Jesus will never take advantage of your vulnerability or weaknesses. You can trust Jesus with your future. In order for your King to show you the kindness He has prepared for you, you have to come to the King and let Him position you at the table.

5
Guilt versus Shame

In the previous chapters, we have briefly approached the difference between guilt and shame. In order to know how to deal with each one, we need to ensure we have a grasp on the distinction between them.

Guilt

Guilt is the action or violation. It is the wrong you did. Guilt is the position or condition of standing where your action has placed you. A person can be found guilty. If you are confessing to something you would say, "I am guilty." You would be describing your state of being.

Shame

Shame is the feeling or pain in your conscience caused by your guilt. You feel shame. You experience it. Shame isn't just felt in your emotions though. Your subconscious experiences a sense of shame. It is a painful feeling that reaches into your thoughts and perceptions. Shame attaches to your memories. You aren't shame. You feel shame.

Guilt and shame can both hinder our approach to God, but in two different ways. Guilt affects the way God can relate to us. Shame affects the way we relate to God. Guilt must be dealt with first and then shame. God always changes our condition of guilt first because it is the cause of the shame. Then, He rid us of our shame. This was the step in God's process that I missed when I first gave my life to Jesus Christ. I allowed God to deal with the guilt. I put faith in the work of the blood to put away my guilt. But the shame was still working in my life. God could reach me, but I was having trouble connecting with God.

Shame stayed hidden in my consciousness. Whenever I felt or experienced the shame, I immediately questioned my guilt. "What did I do? Where did I sin?" I went to the altar to repent a lot in those days. I was repenting for the way I *felt*. I was trying to remove the shame with the same method I used to remove guilt. While the blood is the substance used to remove both guilt and shame, our faith must be exercised toward the sacrifice for guilt and the cleansing of shame.

Everything Jesus did to give us an approach to God was illustrated by the sacrifices and ceremonies of the Old Testament. Under the Old Covenant, there was a difference in the way people dealt with their guilt compared to the way they dealt with the uncleanness caused by the guilt. They had to offer a sacrifice for their guilt. They had different washings for cleansing from things that made them unclean. The sacrifice of the animal's life was a life given for them. They watched and recognized, "This was done for me."

But, the cleansing was an action actually done to them. The blood was sprinkled on them in a ceremony specifically designed for cleansing. They identified with the action as something done to them in order to cleanse them to serve God. Look at the New Testament comparison to this cleansing and the cleansing power of Jesus' blood.

The blood of goats and bulls and the ashes of cows sprinkled on unclean people made their bodies holy and clean. The blood of Christ, who had no defect, does even more. Through the eternal Spirit he offered himself to God and cleansed our consciences from the useless things we had done. Now we can serve the living God (Hebrews 9:13-14 GW)

Jesus died on the cross for us. The sacrifice of His life was given for us. But, that is not the only interaction we are supposed to have with His blood. The blood is supposed to be the cleansing agent for our consciences. We can live free from the embarrassment of our past. We can live free from the humiliation of what we have done. We can live without the torment of what was done to us. When we learn to access this cleansing power by faith in what the Word declares; we can purge, scrub and cleanse our thoughts, emotions and conscience of the shame from our past.

Let's take a closer look at how Jesus dealt with our guilt. Guilt requires judgment. A penalty must be paid for the guilt. Because God is just, He cannot pretend the guilt never happened. It must be dealt with. The penalty for guilt of sin is death. None of us stood a chance because we were all guilty of sin. That is why Jesus left His position in heaven and willingly came to the Earth as a man. He was the only One qualified to die and pay this price. God said in Hebrews 2, Jesus became a man for the following three reasons.

1. To die for every man (Hebrews 2:9).

2. To destroy the one who had the power of death and deliver those under bondage to the fear of death (Hebrews 2:14).

3. To be a merciful and faithful High Priest who can make reconciliation for our sins (Hebrews 2:17).

1. To Die for Every Man

God made two Adams. The word Adam really means "man." I want to use an illustration that applies in today's terminology to help you see this truth. An automobile factory has a prototype of the car they are producing. Every car that comes off the line has the same basic, fundamental characteristics as the prototype or model. While the color may differ, it is still the same automobile. Each car can be customized to have a different stereo, power locks, or a

51

sunroof. Yet, it is the same model of car despite the differences.

God created the first model of man and placed him in the Garden of Eden. God gave the first Adam the instruction to "Be fruitful and multiply." Every person who would be born to this model of man would have his fundamental characteristics. But, before Adam reproduced, He sinned. Sin would be passed on to every person born through his bloodline. Every man, woman, and child was born into the sin-lineage of Adam. We all deserved to die. We all owed our lives in payment for our sins.

Then, God created the second prototype or model of man. The Bible actually calls Him the Last Adam.

Thus it is written, The first man *Adam* became a living being (an individual personality); the *last Adam* (Christ) became a life-giving Spirit [restoring the dead to life] (1 Corinthians 15:45 AMP, *emphasis author's*).

God will never need to create another model because Jesus is perfect. He is the last prototype. When we receive Jesus as Lord of our lives, we are reborn or born again. We are remade according to His model with His characteristics. We now have His attributes of righteousness and holiness. We come off the spiritual assembly line with all of the same qualities as Jesus Christ just like we once exhibited the qualities of the first Adam. We were sinners like the first Adam. Now, we are righteous like the Last Adam.

And just as we have borne the image [of the man] of dust, so shall we and so let us also bear the image [of the Man] of heaven (1 Corinthians 15:49 AMP).

In order to provide that spiritual connection for us to be reborn, Jesus—the Last Adam—had to undo what the first

Adam had done. Jesus had to regain what Adam lost. Jesus had to deal with the guilt that Adam had introduced into the human race. Remember, guilt required judgment. Jesus had to die to pay the penalty. No other person could die and accomplish what the death of God's sinless Son accomplished. Jesus tasted death for every person to provide the opportunity for every person to receive the life of God.

In the Old Testament, the death of the animal on the altar substituted for the death of the person. This substitute only lasted a year. They had to come back with another animal and go through the process of substitution again. The people were only covering their sin because the blood of an animal wasn't valuable enough to pay for their sin to be completely cleansed.

The old system under the law of Moses was only a shadow, a dim preview of the good things to come, not the good things themselves. The sacrifices under that system were repeated again and again, year after year, but they were never able to provide perfect cleansing for those who came to worship (Hebrews 10:1 NLT).

The people were never able to relate to God the way God wanted them to do. The feeling of the guilt was always standing in their way. This shame was deep down in their conscience. They perceived themselves as unacceptable and unclean.

If they could have provided perfect cleansing, the sacrifices would have stopped, for the worshipers would have been purified once for all time, and their feelings of guilt would have disappeared (Hebrews 10:2 NLT).

God's only Son knew this and willingly offered to change the situation. Jesus knew the perfect will of God for every person was a strong, personal relationship. God the Father wanted the liberty to love us as His own children. God the Father wanted every person to have the liberty to enjoy and participate in this relationship without any presence of guilt or sense of shame. This was the will of God. Look at the conversation Jesus had with the Father.

> That is why, when Christ came into the world, he said to God, "You did not want animal sacrifices or sin offerings. But you have given me a body to offer. You were not pleased with burnt offerings or other offerings for sin. Then I said, 'Look, I have come to do your will, O God—as is written about me in the Scriptures'" (Hebrews 10:5-7 NLT).

God loved you and me so extremely, He was willing to offer His only child to bring us into His kingdom and make us His children. This was a sacrifice for God. He invested His very best for us. He gave His all. At the moment God gave Jesus, He had no one else in His family. But, through Jesus Christ, God would be able to have many descendants. Look at this explanation in the book of Isaiah.

> But it was the LORD's good plan to crush him and cause him grief. Yet when his life is made an offering for sin, he will have many descendants. He will enjoy a long life,
> and the LORD's good plan will prosper in his hands. When he sees all that is accomplished by his anguish, he will be satisfied. And because of his experience, my righteous servant will make it possible for many to be counted righteous, for he will bear all their sins. I will give him the honors of a victorious soldier, because he exposed himself to death. He was counted

among the rebels. He bore the sins of many and interceded for rebels (Isaiah 53:10-12 NLT).

Don't you love that? Jesus interceded for rebels! I was one of those rebels! He carried my sin and my shame so I can carry His purity and right standing with God. Jesus made it possible for many to be made righteous. Jesus had to remove our guilt and shame to make us righteous. It pleases God when we can live our life without guilt. Jesus died to purchase that freedom for us.

2. To Destroy the One Who Had the Power of Death and Deliver Those under Bondage to the Fear of Death

Jesus had to die to pay the penalty for sin. When He did, He also destroyed the hold that Satan had over mankind. Jesus fulfilled God's promise to Satan.

> "I will make you and the woman hostile toward each other. I will make your descendants and her descendant hostile toward each other. He will crush your head, and you will bruise his heel" (Genesis 3:15 NLT).

The word "head" represented authority or ability to govern. The devil had become man's governor or lord when Adam sinned. The governing power of the enemy is sin, humiliation and disgrace. Jesus, through His death, destroyed Satan's power to control man. Every person who is born again by receiving Jesus as Lord is completely free from the control of Satan.

> Because God's children are human beings—made of flesh and blood—the Son also became flesh and blood. For only as a human being could he die, and only by dying could he break the power of the devil, who had the power of death. Only in this way could

he set free all who have lived their lives as slaves to the fear of dying (Hebrews 2:14-15 NLT).

This has been done. Jesus already accomplished this liberty and freedom for us. For the person who has made Jesus Lord, eternal life is secure. We have been taken from the kingdom of darkness and placed into the kingdom of God's dear Son. When we leave our body it will be as the Holy Spirit described in Second Corinthians: "To be absent from the body and is to be present with the Lord." We are free from the fear of death.

3. To Be a Merciful and Faithful High Priest Who Can Make Reconciliation for Our Sins

When the blood of the Old Testament animal sacrifice was poured out on the altar it was only the first step in the process. The blood had to continue from the altar into the presence of God and be placed on the mercy seat. The only person who could carry the blood into the Most Holy Place was the person God had appointed as the High Priest. The High Priest was allowed access to the Most Holy Place once every year to cover the sins of the people. His only responsibility at that moment was to place the blood in the presence of God. Instead of a seat of judgment, God has prepared a seat of mercy. When the blood was placed on the mercy seat the sins of the people would be covered. Remember, all of the actions of the Old Testament worship were types and shadows of what Jesus would fulfill. The tabernacle where all of these actions took place was a replica of the original tabernacle that exists in heaven.

For Christ (the Messiah) has not entered into a sanctuary made with [human] hands, only a copy and pattern and type of the true one, but [He has entered] into heaven itself, now to appear in the [very] presence of God on our behalf (Hebrews 9:24 AMP).

If the blood of animals had to be carried by such a specific, qualified representative, how much more important is the One who carries the blood of God's Son in order to place it in on the mercy seat in heaven on our behalf. Jesus was the only One qualified to be the sacrifice and the only One equipped to be the High Priest. Out of all the people in the entire existence of the universe, Jesus is the only One who was sworn into the office of the High Priest with an oath of God Himself.

The Lord has sworn and will not revoke or change it: You are a priest forever, after the manner and order of Melchizedek (Psalm 110:4 AMP).

Jesus is the High Priest for eternity. He was born so that He could die for us. He became a human so, that through death, He could destroy the one who held the power of death and deliver all of us who were in bondage to the fear of death. Jesus was made like us in order to be a merciful and faithful high priest that could make reconciliation for our sins. Jesus is our sacrifice for guilt, the payment for the penalty of sin and the representative who administrates our freedom from shame. What a Savior!

6
The Approach to God

But into the second [division of the tabernacle] none but the high priest goes, and he only once a year, and never without taking a sacrifice of blood with him . . . (Hebrews 9:7a AMP).

The presence of sin demanded the presence of blood in order to approach God. Even though the High Priest was chosen to approach God for the people, he couldn't approach without the blood. We saw in the last chapter, this limited relationship wasn't what the Heavenly Father really wanted. What God really wanted was to have a close, loving relationship with His people. Jesus made a reference to the sacrifice of animal blood and said, "This is not what you really want. I will make possible the kind of relationship you really desire to have with them."

It will help if we take a look back and see the relationship that is referenced by the Lord Jesus in His conversation with the Father. As we examine some major points from the history of the blood as our way to approach God, I want you to focus on the limitations in this relationship compared to the liberty we have through the relationship Jesus has established.

The Blood in the Beginning

The first reference to blood is implied. When Adam and Eve sinned in the Garden of Eden, the glory they were once covered in departed. They hid from God. When He asked them why they were hiding, they told God, "We are naked." God used the skins of animals to cover Adam and Eve. In order to cover the guilt of the first man and woman, blood was shed. Even though they had disobeyed God and caused a separation in the relationship, God still cared for them. In His love, He knew they needed a covering.

The next mention of blood is actually the first example of blood involved in worship. Adam and Eve's sons brought offerings to the Lord.

> When it was time for the harvest, Cain presented some of his crops as a gift to the LORD. Abel also brought a gift—the best of the firstborn lambs from his flock. The LORD accepted Abel and his gift, but he did not accept Cain and his gift. This made Cain very angry, and he looked dejected.
> "Why are you so angry?" the LORD asked Cain. "Why do you look so dejected? You will be accepted if you do what is right. But if you refuse to do what is right, then watch out! Sin is crouching at the door, eager to control you. But you must subdue it and be its master" (Genesis 4:3-7).

The first thing about this story that strikes me is God was talking to them. Specifically, God is coaching Cain about how to approach Him. God wants to accept Cain. But, Cain isn't coming under the covering of blood. Cain wants to approach God with his effort. The problem is Cain's effort cannot wash away the guilt. All of Cain's hard work can't cleanse the shame.

Evidently, God told Cain and Abel the acceptable way to approach Him. The only way for faith to come is by hearing God's Word. In the book of Hebrews, we see that Abel was moved by faith when he brought the sacrifice to God.

> It was by faith that Abel brought a more acceptable offering to God than Cain did. Abel's offering gave evidence that he was a righteous man, and God

showed his approval of his gifts. Although Abel is long dead, he still speaks to us by his example of faith (Hebrews 11:4).

God wasn't showing favoritism to Abel. Abel brought the blood like God had instructed him to do. God was operating within the limits that mankind's guilt had placed on the relationship. Because God is holy, He could not have the interaction that He wanted.

When a person is placed in prison, they have restrictions on the interaction they can have with their family. They have limits on the telephone calls they can make. Often that prisoner has to visit with their family from behind a glass barrier. They have limited time and limited access with the people they love. I think the Heavenly Father felt like He was visiting His children in prison. Guilt held God at a distance.

God loves Cain so much. He speaks to Cain and encourages him to bring the blood. God said, "If you do the right thing, you will be accepted." Listen to the love in that statement. "I want you to be in right standing with me. I have given you a way to cover your guilt. Do the right thing."

The Life Is in the Blood: a Lesson of Substitution

For the life of the body is in its blood. I have given you the blood on the altar to purify you, making you right with the LORD. It is the blood, given in exchange for a life, that makes purification possible (Leviticus 17:11 NLT).

. . . because blood contains life. I have given this blood to you to make peace with me on the altar. Blood is needed to make peace with me (Leviticus 17:11 GW).

God was teaching His people the purpose and reason for the blood. The life is in the blood. The blood is the force of your life. It carries life to every part of your body. If your blood poured out of your body, your life would flow out with it. God said, "I have given you the blood on the altar to purify you." The blood makes peace with God. But it was a temporary solution. Animal blood on earthly altars kept mankind connected to God until the Lamb of God could pour out His blood, carry it to the heavenly altar and permanently secure our approach to the Father.

When the worshippers in the Old Testament brought their lambs to offer to God, they did so with the understanding "This lamb is taking my place." Generally, it was a lamb raised in their flock. They spent time with lamb. The lamb was sweet. It was affectionate. The innocent, little lamb had followed them around as they fed the other animals. The lamb played with their children. Often, the lamb felt like part of the family. To lead the little lamb to the altar was a serious moment. To watch the innocent animal as the priest cut its throat and the blood flowed out onto the altar caused the worshipper to recognize the exchange that was taking place. "This lamb is innocent. I am guilty. The lamb is paying for what I deserve to receive. I am purified by the life of the lamb." Innocence is exchanged for guilt. Every sacrifice was supposed to invoke this thought process.

> The next day John seeth Jesus coming unto him, and saith, Behold the Lamb of God, which taketh away the sin of the world (John 1:29 KJV).

The cross was a form of capital punishment in the days of Jesus Christ. It was reserved for the vilest, hardest criminals who had performed the worst crimes. Many people died on crosses in those times. What made the cross of Jesus Christ any different than the crosses of the criminals?

Jesus wasn't a hardened criminal. He wasn't sent to the cross as punishment for crimes He had committed. Jesus was sent to the cross by the High Priest of His time. The chief priests and temple guards were the ones who took Jesus into custody in the Garden of Gethsemane (Luke 22:52). They took Jesus to the house of the High Priest to accuse Him (Luke 22:54). The High Priest accused Jesus of blasphemy (Matthew 26:65) and had the chief priest and elders take Jesus to Pilate for execution. Jesus was the innocent Lamb taken by the priests and carried to the altar.

The Altar and the Blood

Long before there was a tabernacle or a temple, people still made their approach to God. As long as the people could make an altar, they could worship. Blood given to God is what made the cross of Jesus different from every other cross. It was His innocent, holy blood that produced a supernatural effect. The blood Jesus poured out on the cross changed the cross from plain, ordinary wood into a holy, consecrated altar. During the preparation for the tabernacle, God had instructed Moses how to prepare the altar. Blood offered to God on the altar caused the altar to become holy and caused whatever would touch the altar to be holy.

Purify the altar, and consecrate it every day for seven days. After that, the altar will be absolutely holy, and whatever touches it will become holy (Exodus 29:37 NLT).

Hebrews 13:10 declares, "We have an altar. . . ." We approach that altar where Jesus' life was given, and we receive the substitution. Just like that person who carried their lamb to the tabernacle, we can stand in our faith and see the life that was given in an exchange for our guilt. We can know we are innocent because we have a Lamb.

7

Draw Near

Because Jesus has removed the burden of guilt, we have an access to God that the people of the Old Testament couldn't reach. The people who brought their blood sacrifice to the tabernacle never went beyond the altar. Even the priests who worked in the outer court of the tabernacle couldn't pass into the holiest place where God's presence lived. But, you and I are able to enter the holiest and draw near to God.

> Having therefore, brethren, boldness to *enter into the holiest by the blood* of Jesus,
> By *a new and living way*, which he hath consecrated for us, through the veil, that is to say, his flesh;
> And having an high priest over the house of God;
> *Let us draw near* with a true heart in full assurance of faith, having our hearts sprinkled from an evil conscience, and our bodies washed with pure water (Hebrews 10:19-22 KJV, *emphasis author's*).

We can enter into the holiest place of all: the throne of God's holy presence. We can enter because the blood has made us holy and guilt-free. The word "enter" used in this passage is the word that describes a priest approaching God. When the blood cleanses you from guilt, it is such a complete cleansing that you are pure enough to be considered a priest. You are qualified to minister to the Lord in His holy, heavenly temple. You can bring Him sacrifices of praise. You can offer prayers for your family, friends and even yourself. The blood not only cleanses your guilt. It makes you holy!

The Bible says, "Unto Him that loved us and washed us from our sins in His own blood and has made us kings and priests unto God . . . " (Revelation 1:5-6). The washing of the blood made us kings and priests. That means the blood made you a part of the royal family and at the same time qualified you as priest to minister to God and for God.

In Revelation 7, the Bible says the people who have "washed their robes and made them white in the blood of the Lamb are before the throne of God and serve Him night and day in His temple" (Revelation 7:14-15). What an honor! Think about the privilege. A woman like me who spent years selling my body in sin and wasting years with cocaine-induced paranoia can become so clean and holy as to serve God at His throne in Heaven!

You can enter heaven's holiest location where the King of the Universe is seated in His place of power. Through the blood, you belong there. Through the blood, you can approach Him with a smile on your face. You can approach your Heavenly Father with eagerness to tell Him about your day.

We can have the relationship with God that He has always wanted and have always needed. We can come to our Heavenly Father without shame. Jesus has prepared a new and living way! Our response to this reality is in verse 23: "Draw near. . . ." When our faith grasps the truth of our guiltlessness, we will automatically draw near. God is calling us "Come closer!" Look at this passage from the *God's Word* translation.

Brothers and sisters, because of the blood of Jesus we can now confidently go into the holy place. Jesus has opened a new and living way for us to go through the curtain. (The curtain is his own body.) We have a superior priest in charge of God's house. *We have been sprinkled with his blood to free us from a guilty conscience,* and our bodies have been washed with clean water. So we must continue to come to him with a sincere heart and strong faith (Hebrews 10:19-22 GW, *emphasis author's*).

The sprinkling of the blood is what cleanses the conscience of all shame and any feeling of worthlessness because of yesterday's guilt. God doesn't want you to always feel shame when you talk to Him. He wants your heart to reach for Him, not draw away from Him. It was the shame that caused Adam and Eve to draw back from God's presence. God never yelled at them or threatened to hurt them.

It was the shame that caused me to draw back when I needed God's help the most. When I needed to go straight to the throne of my Heavenly Father and receive strength and healing power for my unborn child, the shame of that abortion caused me to withdraw. The same feeling of worthlessness, that kept me from God for so many years, haunted my mind with images of God blaming me. In my heart, I was afraid that God would blame me. I was already forgiven for that abortion. Jesus had removed the burden of guilt when He gave His life's blood on the altar of the cross. Shame was trespassing in my life, but I didn't know it was there illegally.

Therefore, I let shame continually rehearse my failure until I was convinced I could not go to God for help. I didn't go to God, not with faith or confident expectation. God said, "Draw near, Michelle. Come closer." But, I drew away from God.

In my first marriage, I was a victim to physical abuse. Many times, I was beaten for something I said or even a look I gave. One time my first husband woke me up in the middle of the night to beat me. The man who was supposed to love me would hit me with his fists. I took the blame and believed the lie that I had done something to deserve it. I became so used to that type of treatment that I expected it.

When I married Philip Steele, I didn't know how to disagree without a fight. In the early years of our marriage, whenever we would disagree, I thought he would hit me so I was ready to defend myself. If he raised his voice, I began to brace myself. There were times I ducked my head or pulled back from him because I thought he would hit me. I was responding to the only man who ever really loved me like he was someone else. I was drawing back from him because I didn't know how to act with trust in a relationship.

I did the same thing to my Heavenly Father. I drew back in shame. I retreated from His presence and became a victim again. I didn't know how to act around God without guilt. If I wasn't apologizing or repenting, I didn't know what to say. I wasn't sure how to be comfortable or confident around God. I needed to cleanse my conscience!

For years before I met Jesus Christ, I drove illegally. I lost my driver's license because I was in an accident without insurance. I had multiple tickets and fines that I had never paid. Add to the scenario the fact I always had marijuana and some pills with me. Many times, the tags didn't belong to the car and I never kept insurance. Every time I got pulled over by the police, I was in trouble for something.

After I received Jesus as Lord, I not only cleaned up from prostitution, crime, and drugs, I went and got insurance and had my driver's license reinstated. The first time a police car got in the lane behind me, my hands started to sweat. My heart started racing and my stomach got butterflies. I watched my speed and started to dart my eyes from the road to the rearview mirror. Then, I thought to myself *What are you worried about?* I was perfectly legal! My tags, registration, and insurance were intact. No drugs or alcohol were in the car. I was sober! If they pulled me over, I wasn't going to jail! I was so excited!

What stopped my heart from racing? What stopped the butterflies and the stomach from being tied in knots? It was the realization that things were different. It was the revelation of what is compared to what was. I was so used to the way of guilt. I was used to it. I knew how to act guilty. Shame was familiar to me. When I realized everything had changed, I felt different. I acted different.

Don't wait until you feel forgiven. Being forgiven isn't really something you feel. So don't wait until you feel righteous. It is not a feeling. You are what Jesus made you. You aren't what you feel. Feelings are unstable sources of information, especially when they are motivated by past experiences. It is vital that you focus on the truth of who you are and the relationship you have with God through Jesus Christ. You cannot approach God by any other way. You can't approach God on your merit or education. You can't approach God with your effort or emotions. Come to God through the new and living way. Come to the Father through the blood of Jesus Christ.

The blood has the power to draw you closer to God.

But now through Christ Jesus you, who were once far away, have been brought near by the blood of Christ (Ephesians 2:13 GW).

If you want to grow in your relationship with God, begin to build a strong faith in the power of Jesus' blood. Begin to think about and focus on the access, boldness, and courage His blood can provide. Jesus' blood opened a path for you to go straight to God's throne. When you build faith in this truth, you will begin to sense your righteousness.

The exchange or substitution we have discussed included an exchange of unrighteousness for righteousness. You can draw near as a royal child of God and a priest of God because Jesus gave you His righteousness. Righteousness means "right standing." It is the ability to stand in God's presence without any sense of condemnation, inferiority, or guilt. You don't feel righteousness. It is not something you can locate with your physical senses. It is a spiritual condition or force.

You can't locate a molecule with your natural eye. It requires a microscope to find it. You can't see the emotions or thoughts of another person. It requires communication to discover what they are thinking. You can't find righteousness with your feelings. Righteousness is found with your faith.

When Jesus cleanses you with His blood, you are made righteous at that very moment. If you cussed someone out in the morning and give your life to Jesus Christ that evening, you are 100 percent righteous the moment you received Jesus as Lord. The day I received Jesus as Lord of my life, I put a needle in my arm and shot Dilaudid in my veins earlier that morning. What I had done didn't stop Jesus from making the exchange in my life.

> For he hath made him to be sin for us, who knew no sin; that we might be made the righteousness of God in him (2 Corinthians 5:21 KJV).

Jesus, who never sinned, was made to be sin. Jesus never committed a sin. But, God placed all sin on Jesus in an instant. He became sin for us so that we could be made righteous. I was made righteous even though I couldn't feel it. If you asked Jesus to forgive you, and you submitted your life to Him, you were made righteous even if you didn't know it. If you commit a sin after being righteous, you can confess your sin to Jesus. He will forgive you and cleanse you again from all unrighteousness. He makes you 100 percent pure all over again!

Righteousness isn't a word used very often outside of church. I didn't understand the concept of righteousness when I first started attending church and reading my Bible.

An easy way to think of righteousness is to use the illustration of a landlord and a tenant. If you rented an apartment from an apartment complex and you paid your rent on time every month, you wouldn't feel embarrassed at all if you had to request a repair in your apartment. On the other hand, if you were three months behind on your rent, you might feel intimidated about asking to have the maintenance crew come work on your busted pipe. The unrighteous position of being late on your rent causes shame. If you were paid up on your rent or in a righteous position, you would have confidence and boldness to ask for what is provided as part of your contract.

When you are aware of the price Jesus paid, you realize your position of righteousness or right standing with God. You realize this righteousness is not based on your actions whether good or bad. Your position of right standing with God is based on or determined by what Jesus has done. You have to go to the Word of God to access faith in what Jesus has done.

For with the heart man believeth unto righteousness; and with the mouth confession is made unto salvation (Romans 10:10 KJV).

Righteousness is produced by faith, and it operates in your heart. You *know* you are righteous because you see it in God's Word. If you wait until you *feel* righteous, you will never operate the righteousness and receive the liberty we have been talking about. For years, I suffered in frustration. I was continually trying to be what I already was by Jesus' blood. I was trying to do in my human effort and ability what Jesus had already finished in His sinless, selfless sacrifice.

If my husband purchased a gift card for one thousand dollars at the local mall and left it at customer service for me to pick up, I could take a trip to the mall and shop in any store I wanted. The provision would be supplied. The money would be waiting on me. I just need to know about the provision. Let's say my husband told me, "There is one thousand dollars on a gift card with your name on it. Just go get it and purchase what you need or want." Instead of running to the mall, I started thinking to myself, "I don't feel like I deserve to spend one thousand dollars on myself. I don't feel worthy to spend his money. I haven't been the perfect wife. I burned dinner last night. I ruined his favorite soccer jersey when I washed it. Even though I really need clothes and my shoes are worn out, I am not deserving of his gift."

Before we go any further, I want to go on record to state that this would never happen. I would never, under any circumstance, excuse my way out of a shopping trip. When my husband wants to bless me with new clothes, I am always ready to receive! Philip, when you read this, you don't have to get a gift card and leave it at the customer service counter for me. Cash is always great, and I will always appreciate your willingness to bless me with shopping trips. Now, back to my illustration.

The shopping trip in our illustration of a gift given is not based on performance. It is not about the recipient. The gift is the expression of the giver. It is not something that has to be earned or deserved. It is provided by love. The receiver only has to believe in the love and the gift in order to receive what is provided. All I would have to do is say, "Thank you!" and go participate in what has been provided.

Righteousness cannot be earned. It is not yours when you deserve it. It is yours even though you don't deserve it. It is a gift. If you had to deserve it, it would not be a gift. If you had to qualify for it, it would not be a gift.

> For if by one man's offence death reigned by one;
> much more they which receive abundance of grace
> and of the *gift of righteousness* shall reign in life by

one, Jesus Christ (Romans 5:17 KJV, *emphasis author's*).

Righteousness is so important. Let me remind you of this. Jesus was in heaven with the Father. He looked at the relationship between God and fallen mankind. Jesus saw how difficult it was for God the Father to be separated from us. Jesus watched the suffering and frustration as mankind tried to know their purpose and potential without an intimate relationship with the One who created them. As people covered their sins every year and withdrew from God's presence, Jesus stepped up to the throne. He said, "You aren't able to show these people your love and favor like you really want to. You have to love them from a distance. These people aren't able to experience your goodness because guilt and shame is in the way. Send me, Father. I want to do your will. Prepare me a body and I will offer it to pay the ransom. I will free mankind and you can bring them back into the family. They can be your children. They can have the keys back to the house and come to the throne to love you. You can love them again without holding anything back. We can restore them to authority and give them position in the kingdom business. It will be better than it was before!"

God doesn't want us hiding in the back of the palace, cowering and embarrassed to be in heaven. He wants us walking through His house like a child in Daddy's house. Any loving parent would want their child to feel secure and confident in their relationship. What would you think if a person's child was always fearful and withdrawn when that parent was around? What would you think if the child walked in the kitchen and said, "I don't deserve to eat dinner tonight"? I didn't finish cleaning my room, and I failed my spelling test. I am unworthy to have a glass of milk. I didn't earn the right to sleep under this roof tonight.

I guess I will sleep outside in the doghouse. I don't feel righteous enough to accept your love"?

Jesus became sin to make you righteous. You are righteous because His blood cleansed you and made you holy. You are made near or brought into relationship with God because of the blood. You had a spiritual blood transfusion when you touched the altar, the cross. Whatever or whoever touches the cross is made holy. With your faith, you touched the cross of Jesus Christ and now you have access to God. You are righteous. Receive it and walk in it!

The Heavenly Father is calling you to draw near with a heart assured of His love. "Come closer."

8
Do You Have Your I.D.?

- The word "identity" is defined as the condition of being oneself and not another. It is the state or fact of being the same one as described. If the police officer or TSA agent asks you for a form of I.D. you show them a document or license that describes you. On the driver's license, for example, it declares your age, weight, color of eyes and hair. The details describe you.

What information are you consulting to confirm your identity? Are you looking at the past for details to describe you? If so, you might say, "I am a failure because I had a divorce." You might look at the choices of your adult children and say, "I am a terrible person because my son is in prison." Do your mistakes tell you who you are? Are they an accurate, reliable indicator of who you really are?

Are you looking at the way other people have treated you to confirm your identity? If so, you might say, "I am unlovable because my father left us." You might believe, "I am not a good woman because my husband had an affair." You might think, "There is something wrong with me because that person molested me when I was just a boy." Do the actions and treatment of other people dictate the way you perceive yourself?

Are you consulting your feelings and emotions to locate your identity? If so, you may be changing your identity constantly. Unless your emotions and feelings are governed by God's Word and guided by your born-again spirit, they are untrustworthy. "Do I feel like God loves me? Do I feel accepted by God? Do I feel righteous?" How would you know? What does it feel like to be accepted or righteous? Are you expecting the same goose bumps or thrills you experienced before?

Listen, I wake up every morning married. I don't always feel married. What does "married" feel like? I am married because of a covenant I entered into with Philip Steele. We have legal documents and a verbal commitment. It is a decision Philip and I made. We are married even on the days we don't feel like it. If we disagree, we are still married.

You are a righteous, covenant child of the Lord God Almighty because you chose to receive Jesus Christ as your Savior and Lord. No matter what your past says, your identity is based on that decision. No matter how other people treat you or how they have treated you in the past, your identity is secure in Jesus your Lord. No matter what your feelings and emotions say, your identity can only be found in Christ your Lord.

You received new legal documents to identify yourself in Christ. If your circumstance or situation asks you to prove who you are, pull out your new I.D. and identify yourself in Christ.

Therefore if any man be in Christ, he is a new creature: old things are passed away; behold, all things are become new (2 Corinthians 5:17 KJV).

The Greek word for creature gives the understanding of a new creation that never existed before. Jesus called it being "born again." You are born of the Spirit. The person I am today has never prostituted or shot dope. I am a new creation. The old has passed away. Michelle B.C. (Before Christ) participated in the crime and addiction. I am now Michelle A.D. (After Deliverance) made pure and holy and righteous. Look at this translation of the same verse.

This means that anyone who belongs to Christ has become a new person. The old life is gone; a new life has begun! (2 Corinthians 5:17 NLT).

Where did the old life go? How did a new life start? Where can I find the legal documents to prove the old life of guilt is actually gone? Is there a record or any proof? Do I have a death certificate to prove the Michelle B.C. is actually dead? Do I have a birth certificate to prove the new life has come? I do! I have a death certificate and a new birth certificate. You have to be able to read the language of faith if you want to see understand it.

If I wanted to obtain my birth certificate, I have to go to the courthouse or government office and locate the document that testifies to my birth. In the spiritual arena, we have a legal place to locate our records. The documents testify to our death and birth. They are spiritual witnesses that give testimony to our life change. The faith that overcomes the world is anchored in these three testimonies.

So there are three witnesses in heaven: the Father, the Word and the Holy Spirit, and these three are One; and there are three witnesses on the earth: the Spirit, the water, and the blood; and these three agree [are in unison; their testimony coincides] (1 John 5:7-8 AMP).

Here on the earth, we have three witnesses or faith documents to identify us. The Spirit, the water and the blood are speaking and giving accurate testimony for who we are, who we belong to and when the change took place in our lives. They are written in the language of faith, so practice reading in faith as we look closer at these documents.

The Spirit

Just think how much more the blood of Christ will purify our consciences from sinful deeds so that we can worship the living God. For *by the power of the eternal Spirit*, Christ offered himself to God as a perfect sacrifice for our sins (Hebrews 9:14 NLT, *emphasis author's*).

The Holy Spirit motivated and strengthened Jesus Christ as He faced the cross. The Holy Spirit was there. He is a faithful witness. When He takes the stand in heaven's courtroom, there is no doubt the words He speaks are truth. When shame says you aren't saved, the Holy Spirit stands up and declares, "I was there when you were crucified for your sin. You have already paid the price."

Wait a minute! Jesus was crucified, not you! You never went to the cross. But, Jesus died for you. He was crucified in your place. So, by reason of His action, you have been crucified. When you receive it—as done for you—you so completely identify with the sacrifice that it is done to you. You have been crucified! This is how Paul said it.

I have been crucified with Christ [in Him I have shared His crucifixion]; it is no longer I who live, but Christ (the Messiah) lives in me; and the life I now live in the body I live by faith in (by adherence to and reliance on and complete trust in) the Son of God, Who loved me and gave Himself up for me (Galatians 2:20 AMP).

When you identify with what Jesus has done for you to the point you receive it, you will know the old, guilt-ridden miserable you died on the cross with Jesus Christ. You have been crucified! You have to know you've been crucified.

Knowing this, that our old man is crucified with him, that the body of sin might be destroyed, that henceforth we should not serve sin (Romans 6:6 KJV, *emphasis author's*).

The Amplified Bible says, "We know that our old (unrenewed) self was nailed to the cross with Him. . . ."

In the *God's Word* translation it reads, "We know that the person we used to be was crucified with him. . . ."

The old you is passed away. The Holy Spirit was there to witness it. He won't lie to you. Your feelings will lie to you. The circumstance will lie to you. The Holy Spirit is the Spirit of Truth. He can't lie. He says you were crucified with Christ. That means you should say what the Holy Spirit says about you. You need to testify, "I have been crucified and my old self is dead. I can't carry shame for a guilt that has been paid for. I have a death certificate for the old me."

The Water

If someone has a death certificate proving they are dead, it seems right that we should a location where they have been buried. You have proof of where your old self was buried.

Romans 6:4 tells you where you were buried: "Therefore we are buried with him by baptism into death" (KJV).

In the *God's Word* translation it says, "When we were baptized into his death, we were placed into the tomb with him." Did you know you have been buried in the tomb with Jesus? The Bible doesn't lie. This is the witness on the Earth that testifies of your true identity. You have been crucified and buried!

The Blood

The blood is a legal witness. In today's courtroom, people are found guilt or innocent by the testimony of DNA from blood samples. It is considered a reputable source of proof and evidence. You have Jesus blood as your evidence. What is the testimony of the blood saying about you?

> Now the God of peace, that brought again from the dead our Lord Jesus, that great shepherd of the sheep, through the blood of the everlasting covenant (Hebrews 13:20 KJV).

The *God's Word* translation says the God of Peace brought Jesus "back to life through the blood." The blood gave God the legal right to raise Jesus from the dead. God came and dealt with Adam's mistake legally and within the parameters of His own Word. The blood sealed and made legal the new, everlasting covenant. It is the covenant or contract of your new life. The blood of Jesus Christ is your birth certificate. It marks the day you were resurrected from the dead!

You were crucified with Christ. You were buried with Christ. You were resurrected to a new life. The blood is the legal witness or evidence that speaks this truth. You have a resurrected life. You can live His life instead of the guilty, shame-filled life of your past.

> We were buried therefore with Him by the baptism into death, so that just as Christ was raised from the dead by the glorious [power] of the Father, so we too might [habitually] live and behave in newness of life. For if we have become one with Him by sharing a death like His, we shall also be [one with Him in *sharing*] *His resurrection* [by a new life lived for God] (Romans 6:4-5 AMP, *emphasis author's*).

The blood testifies you have a new life. You aren't limited to human ability in this life. It is the Anointed One and His anointing living in you. You have the nature of God in you now. God has given you His strength, wisdom, and ability to help you every moment of your life. God is working in you.

Get your faith documents out and meditate on them. Re-identify yourself. You aren't a product of what happened to you. You aren't what other people said about you. You aren't what you did or what you didn't do. You are who the Spirit, the water, and the blood say you are. You are crucified with Christ, buried into His death, and resurrected into His new life.

9
Everything Has Changed

And they sang a new song with these words:

"You are worthy to take the scroll and break its seals
and open it. For you were slaughtered, and your
blood has ransomed people for God from every tribe
and language and people and nation. And you have
caused them to become a Kingdom of priests for our
God. And they will reign on the earth" (Revelation
5:9-10 NLT).

In heaven, the focus of victory is on the blood of Jesus
Christ. When the apostle John is describing his experience
in heaven he describes Jesus in these words: a Lamb as it
had been slain or a Lamb that had been slaughtered. John
knew Jesus as his teacher, his leader, his beloved Master.
Seeing Jesus in His position as the One who has prevailed
to open the Will of God for mankind, John describes Him
as a slaughtered Lamb.

If the worship in heaven is centered upon the Lamb,
and the songs they sing are exalting the blood and the One
who poured out His blood, how much more should we give
our attention to Jesus' blood in our lives on Earth? There is
a verse in the book of Revelations which talks about our
future. It says the blood is the weapon we use to overcome
our adversary.

And they overcame him by the blood of the Lamb,
and by the word of their testimony; and they loved
not their lives unto the death (Revelation 12:11 KJV).

Jesus overcame and prevailed over the enemy with His blood. We overcome and prevail against the enemy with His blood. You cannot fight this battle alone. You must soak yourself in the knowledge of His blood and what it has done in you. When your strongest praise is motivated by the change the blood has made in your life, you are just beginning to understand what an impact the blood has had on eternity.

When the Son of God was nailed to the altar of the cross and His blood poured out of His body, everything in the world changed. Literally, everything in the world changed. Before that moment, mankind was separated from the life of God. Before that moment, our future was locked in misery because of guilt and shame. The blood of Jesus Christ changed our lives. We should see history in two parts. There is the segment of time before the blood of Jesus and there is the segment of time after the blood of Jesus was shed.

If you have received Jesus as Lord, that should be the separation in your story. This is the before and after picture in my life. Everything is different in the part of my life the blood is applied to. Like a person who has lost weight and had a total-life makeover, we should be able to say, "This is my life after I lost the guilt and Jesus cleansed me of the shame." Everyone will be shocked at the difference!

A lot of people who hear my testimony are shocked when they actually see me. I have had people say to me, "You don't look like you have been through the things you have been through." When people see my television program, they are shocked to find out the woman preaching on television once sold her body for twenty dollars. They are surprised to know that I attempted suicide. People are astounded that I was a junkie.

The thing that really surprises people is the fact that God would still use someone who was once a prostitute, an addict, and a criminal. If you know the supernatural ability of the blood to really change a person's life, it shouldn't be a surprise. If you believe the blood changed eternity, it isn't a surprise. The people who are singing the victory song of the blood in heaven are not surprised at what God has done in my life.

I want you to know the blood of Jesus in such a way that it rids you of every shame. I want you to be so open with God and not withdraw from Him. Even if God speaks to you about things you can change, you don't draw back. Instead, you draw near to Him.

You can't stand in a prayer line to make this possible. Just reading this book won't make it possible. The best sermon in the world won't make it possible. Receiving and welcoming into your life the shed blood of Jesus Christ is the only thing that makes this liberty possible.

In your body, the blood is constantly working for you. It carries oxygen to the cells of your body. It continues to feed life and nourish it every day. The blood of Jesus will constantly bring His victory to every part of your life.

As I close, I want to challenge you in your relationship with God. If you have always disqualified yourself because of your lifestyle, your guilt, or your unworthiness, stop playing that excuse card. Jesus qualifies you through His blood.

Pray this prayer and accept the sacrifice:

Heavenly Father, I come to you in the name of Jesus. You said in your Word, "Whoever calls on the name of the Lord shall be saved." I am calling on you. I ask Jesus to be the Lord of my life. I believe what He did on the cross was for me and I receive it. I confess Jesus is the Lord of my life and I believe You raised Him from the dead. Thank You for saving me. Thank You for removing all the guilt of my old life. I receive Your new life and I am free from guilt and shame.

If you are saved and live a frustrated life of shame, from this moment on, refuse to allow shame to remain in your life. It is not there by God's design. It is there illegally. Purge your conscience with the blood. Pray this prayer and apply faith in the blood to that area.

Heavenly Father, I come to you in the name of my Lord Jesus Christ. I know when I made Jesus my Savior, You removed the guilt of sin and my past mistakes. I recognize shame is present in my life and I choose to resist it in Jesus' name. According to your Word, the blood of Jesus is so powerful it can purge and completely cleanse my conscience. By faith, I apply that truth to my mind, my emotions and my conscience. I am clean from all shame. The blood of Jesus cleanses me. I am righteous in the eyes of God through the blood of my Savior. Thank you Lord! I rejoice in You!

If you have prayed either of these prayers, I believe your life will never be the same. If you have received a greater knowledge about Jesus' blood, walk in the light of that knowledge. Apply these truths to your life and teach them to your family and friends. I would love to rejoice with you about your freedom from shame. Please take a moment to contact me and let me know how this truth has touched your life.

If you would like prayer for a family member, a friend or yourself, please send your prayer request. Our prayers are powerful weapons for God's glory. The power of Jesus' name, the application of Jesus' blood, and the agreement of prayer are weapons more powerful than methamphetamine addiction, anorexia, or depression. Send me your prayer requests, and let's get in agreement.

Faith Builders International & Michelle Steele Ministries
P.O. Box 452
De Soto, KS 66018

1-913-583-1670

www.michellesteeleministries.com

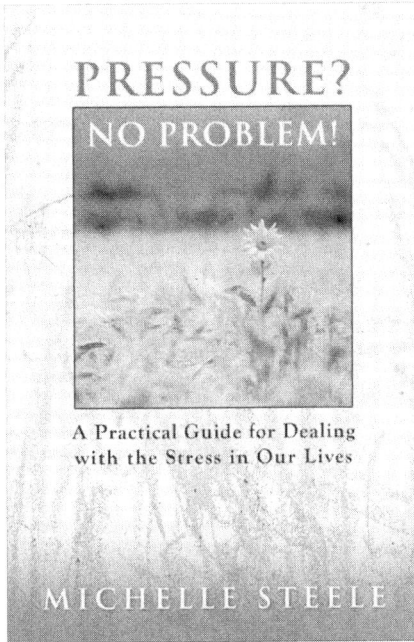

Pressure? No Problem!

The pressure you are facing today has a purpose. It has come to steal your peace, paralyze your faith and hinder your progress. It is designed by your adversary to wear you down, make you weary, and cause you to quit. The enemy wants to make you change your mind. But God is on your side! He has equipped you to rise above the resistance and defeat the pressure.

Soft-cover book $12

Now You See Me Now You Don't

Life may have positioned you in a pit. The situation may have you in a stranglehold. Your past may be holding you hostage. Your present circumstance may be threatening to break you. Find out how you can soar above the storm and break free from the barriers in your life. It isn't a magic trick. It is not an illusion. It is a transformation. In her book "Now You See Me, Now You Don't!" Michelle Steele will equip you to leave the situation and enter the revelation!
Soft-cover book $12

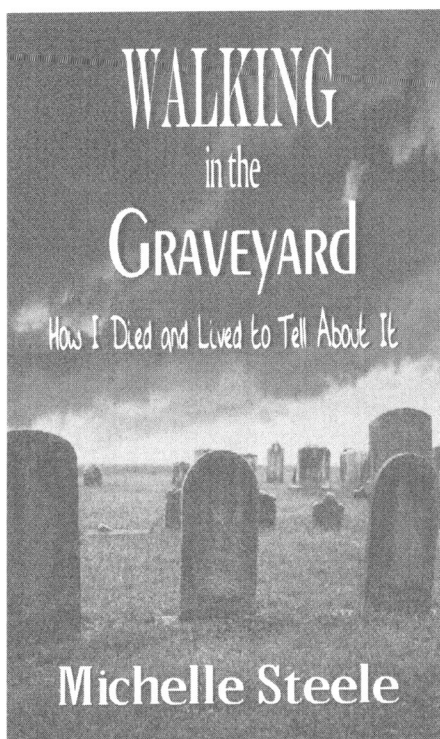

Walking in the Graveyard

As a young, teenage girl, I made wrong decision after wrong decision. I made trouble at home, trouble at school, and trouble in my family. The real trouble was the self-destructing pain on the inside of me. From the age of fifteen until I turned twenty-three, I ran through the tombs and hid in the mountains of drug addiction, prostitution, and criminal activity. My name is Michelle Steele and this is my story.
Soft-cover book $12

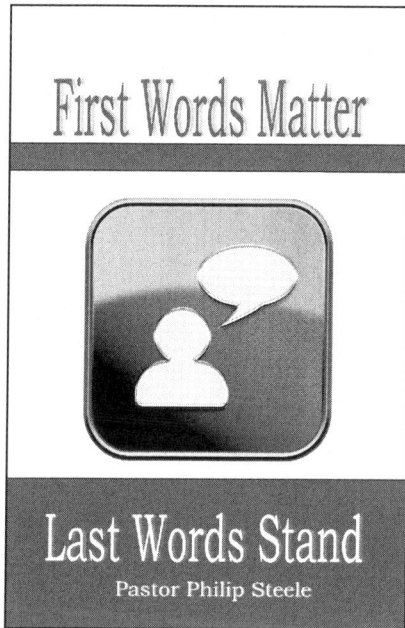

First Words Matter...Last Words Stand
Pastor Philip Steele

Pastor Philip Steele will teach you the importance of the first words you speak in any situation. You will discover how those words set your course and how words will keep you on track with the plan of God! Words are not just meaningless sounds coming out of our mouths. Words are containers of either the life and power of God or the death and destruction of the curse.-Philip Steele
Soft-cover book $8

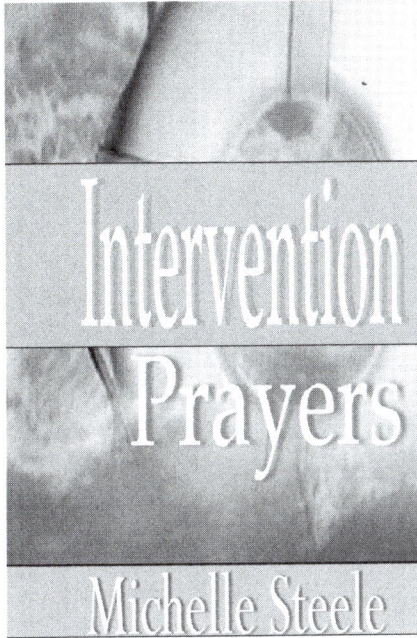

Intervention Prayers

If someone you love is addicted to drugs, wasting away
with an eating disorder or under bondage to any lifestyle that is threatening to take their life, you can set up
an intervention! This prayer devotional is full of inspira-
tion and instruction to help you pray for someone you
love. Your prayers are tools and instruments of intervention that God will utilize to open a hardened heart.

Soft-cover book $10

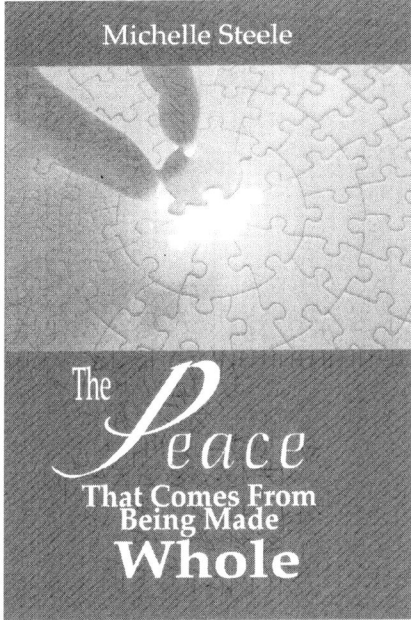

The Peace That Comes From Being Made Whole

Many people define "peace" as freedom from chaos or calamity. God has an entirely different concept. God's idea of peace is "Nothing-Missing and Nothing-Broken." The Lord wants us to have "The Peace That Comes From Being Made Whole." Michelle Steele explains this super-natural power of peace and how you can access it in your life.

Soft-cover book $10

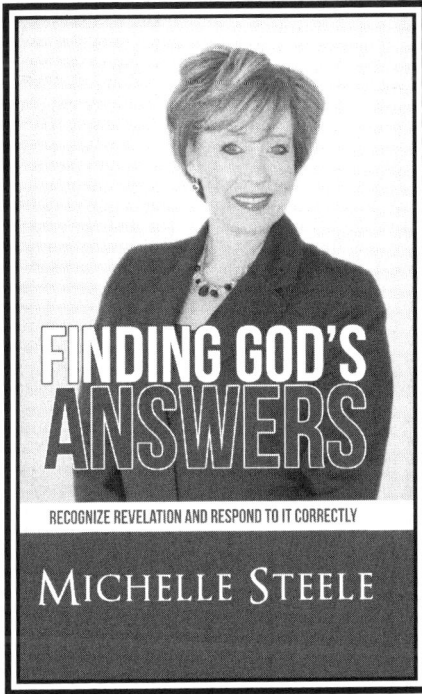

Finding God's Answers

God is not hiding His answers from us. The Lord wants you to find His answers. But, God's answers are spiritual. In order to locate the answer, we have to use the spiritual-reception equipment He provides. I this book you will learn:

- How to recognize revelation and respond correctly
- How to remain tethered to the Truth
- How to avoid the mind-blinding technique of the enemy and much more!

Soft-cover book $12

101